J

AUTHOR OF "7 POWERFUL TECHNIQUES FOR EFFECTIVE SUBCONSCIOUS COMMUNICATION"!

BATTLING INVISIBLE ENEMIES

FACING YOUR INNER STRUGGLES HEAD ON

Copyright © 2018 by Jay Maymi

All rights reserved. Printed in the United States of America. No part of this book may be used or reproduced in any manner whatsoever without written permission except in the case of brief quotations embodied in critical articles or reviews.

Some names and identifying details have been changed to protect the privacy of individuals.

For information, visit:
thejaymaymi.com
contact@thejaymaymi.com

Cover design and Editing by Ivette Maymi
ISBN 13: 978-0-692-79311-4

1st Edition: November 2018
2nd Edition: January 2021

JAY MAYMI

Author of "7 Powerful Techniques for Effective Subconscious Communication"

BATTLING INVISIBLE ENEMIES

FACING YOUR INNER STRUGGLES HEAD ON

TABLE OF CONTENTS

AUTHOR'S THOUGHTS 9

PREFACE 13

INTRODUCTION 19

CHAPTER 1 – DEFINING INVISIBLE ENEMIES 25

CHAPTER 2 – KNOW YOUR ENEMY'S OBJECTIVES 33

CHAPTER 3 – WHEN ATTACKS CAN OCCUR 39

CHAPTER 4 – THE DOWNWARD SPIRAL MODEL OF

                INVISIBLE ENEMY ATTACKS 51

                PHASE 1 – THE SETUP 54

                PHASE 2 – THE KNOCKOUT 63

CHAPTER 5 – DEVELOPING YOUR I.E.D.S. 77

CHAPTER 6 – IN CLOSING 95

REVIEWS - 101

There are many people I could dedicate this book to because their support has been invaluable. I could mention my parents, my children, my friends and colleagues.

However, the one person that deserves this book dedication above anyone is the one who has seen me battle invisible enemies up close these last 17 years. My beautiful wife, Ivette, has been my greatest supporter, cheerleader, and partner in <u>everything</u> I do.

I love you!

"...The mind is its own place and in itself, can make a Heaven of Hell, a Hell of Heaven."

John Milton

"...No man is free who is not master of himself."

Epictetus

AUTHOR'S THOUGHTS

The success of this book has been nothing short of astounding. Now, let me define my meaning of success. When I initially began writing this draft for this book, it was basically for me. It was my way to address some of my head trash therapeutically. I had often read from many credible people that personal therapy can come in the form of writing. Specifically, writing to yourself. This technique is quite powerful because you take yourself "out of the picture" and write about the person you see and the challenges or struggles they are facing. This helps you become almost disengaged and thereby brutally honest and non-partisan in your observation. There is practically a clarity that you did not have before. It also allows you to see what you could not see or understand while in the middle of you being you. Does this make sense to you? Can you see how that can happen? It's a wonderful procedure that I would highly recommend doing when necessary to do so.

When my draft became the book, I shared it with just a few people who immediately resonated with the book and strongly recommended that I make this my next full-fledged project, marketing it to the world. They felt that this was a work that was direly needed and would change lives for the better. They were right. I knew they would be. The book has become, for me, a success not because of the number of books sold. Sales is not just the only way to measure the success of anything. It's just a way to measure how many of one thing people have purchased. In my opinion, success is by how many lives were impacted by the product or service bought. In this case, this book. To date, if I never sold another book, I would declare this book to have been a complete success. After reading it, the people who have come forth shared how the book has dramatically helped them with their inner struggles is a testimony to the book's success. It is positively impacting and influencing lives. I am excited and grateful for that.

So, what can I share with you as you begin reading this book and, hopefully, embark on your battle that will aid in your ultimate victory? Having now been on the other side of battles (they still come but far and few) and having spoken with a large ration of the book's readers, there are a few things you can do. First, you have to take this seriously. The battles that we face with invisible enemies (I explain what invisible enemies are further in the book) are real battles. They start as daily, meaningless skirmishes but immediately surmount into battles if they are not addressed. These battles carry the potential for casualties. Your dreams, desires, potential, joy, confidence, energy, relationships, and freedom become those casualties. With so much at stake, it is not something to take lightly whatsoever. You truly have to stand guard at the doorway of your mind.

As a second point, be relentless about not only winning the battles (if you end up in one) but becoming wiser in the process. Once you know how to defeat your enemy, shame on you if you don't take tactical notes, become more aware, and learn from the process so that you make it very difficult for any future significant invisible enemy assaults. This is how you ensure that future invisible enemy attacks will not stand a chance of penetrating your mind, spirit, and emotions and, thereby, disrupting your life and worthwhile plans.

Lastly, celebrate the victories. Be sure to take time to reflect on the triumph and store it in memory. Do you know why this is so important? This is how you can remind yourself at the conscious and subconscious level that you've faced battles in the past and have WON! This recognition and remembrance is a powerful advantage you will have because you'll know confidently that you've been victorious in the past and so shall be again. This will downgrade any force that the invisible enemies may mount against you.

May VICTORY always be yours!

PREFACE

Many years ago, a young Spanish couple living in NYC took the subway train to the child adoption agency. Earlier in the day, they had been notified that an adoption opportunity had become available to them. Even though they already had a young daughter, the couple became very excited about the idea of parenting an adopted child. They could not get there fast enough. After experiencing two consecutive miscarriages and with very little hope of ever conceiving naturally again, the dream of becoming parents seemed like answered prayer. Upon arriving and meeting with the case manager, they received quite an unexpected announcement and offer. There was indeed an opportunity to adopt that day, except it would not be one child but two. Twins! You can imagine the surprise when they were presented with the offer. The case manager gave them the option to adopt only one if they chose to or be placed back on a waiting list. Considering the difficult economic situation that this young couple newly arrived from Puerto Rico were already facing, it would have been entirely understandable if they decided to either wait for another adoption opportunity or adopt just one of the twins. No one would have blamed them. After all, it would have meant that the mother would have to quit her factory job to tend to 3 children. The father would have to take up a second job to replace the wife's income.

However, on that day, the young couple walked away with a set of three-day-old twin boys. The thought of separating two brothers never crossed their minds. Although they knew that it would not be a cakewalk raising twin boys, the immediate love and compassion they felt for those babies overshadowed their concerns. The years that followed were void of anything extravagant in nature nor luxuries. There were no vacations. No fancy accommodations. No name brand clothing. A challenging neighborhood in the Spanish Harlem hood, their residence was at the "Spanish Harlem Ritz," also known as the NYC Taft Projects. Very few birthday parties. No Whole Foods, but just enough food.

However, there was an abundance of love, support, encouragement, and a home. What more could an adopted kid want? I know this couple well, for they are my parents.

This wonderful upbringing became the breeding ground for my desire to pursue a life of meaningful purpose, high achievement, quality living, and success. It served as the platform that created an entrepreneurial fire within me to pursue a life where I could impact, influence, inspire, and instruct others for their good and, hence, the interest of the rest of the world. These early years impregnated me with ambitions, goals, and a desire for peak performance and extraordinary accomplishments. Realizing that I was given a great chance at life by being one of the fortunate ones adopted into a loving home, I knew that my calling was to be somebody special and not take this opportunity lightly. As such, my entrepreneurial life began by necessity. Like anyone my age, I wanted to afford a new pair of Adidas sneakers. Jordache jeans (I know, I know, I just dated myself. Please stop laughing) and have pocket money that my father could simply not afford to give me.

By age 13, my brother Joe and I decided to collect bottles and cans and cash them in for the nickels they were worth. This was easy to do because we lived only a few blocks away from Central Park. There was always an abundance of empty cans and bottles for the taking, especially after the weekend's baseball and softball games. We were amazed that no one else had the foresight to realize that all these nickels were lying there on the ground, ready to be picked up. I learned my first entrepreneurial lesson; while some will see poop, others will see profit. We saw profit. Well, I can tell you that it felt good to have on a pair of brand-new Adidas and Jordache jeans, hot pressed with the seam running down the middle of each leg. I mean, I was the man! What felt great about it was that I was able to buy them with my own money. The entrepreneurial bug had infected me, and so my journey began.

In the years that followed, I expressed my entrepreneurial spirit in tax preparation work, the entertainment industry, personal fitness training, real estate, financial services, and ministry. I became an author of books and sales training courses, a national keynote speaker, and a personal development coach. I am no stranger to the challenges and battles that I have written about in this book. This book is not written strictly from an academic perspective but from a hands-on one, as well. I have been in the trenches of these battles with invisible enemies. I have worked with those in the same struggles. The battles are real. If you are in a battle, currently or often, this book will equip you to face your inner struggles head-on with more victory than before. If you have seen your conflicts consistently rob you of your joy, peace of mind, and success, then this book will help you regain some of your lost hope and strength back. If you claim to have never been in a battle, get ready because you are heading for one. This book will help you create defense systems so that your invisible enemies will have very little success in sucking you into those life-draining and destiny-crushing battles. I have been in more battles than I care to count. However, they have made me stronger in the end. The same will happen for you.

To your victory!

INTRODUCTION

As someone who has the ability and calling to inspire, influence, impact, and instruct countless others, I must be very analytical in what I present to my followers. This due diligence is always warranted so that what I confidently introduce to my customers is relevant and high-quality content filled with life, career, business, health, and relationship-changing potential. When the inspiration came upon me to write this book, I did not question it whatsoever. Of all the topics that I could have written about, this one I felt would make the most impact in the lives of millions who are also battling invisible enemies but do not know it.

I have discovered a few everyday success-hindering struggles that many face throughout my professional career, personal life, and experiences with friends, family, clients, and colleagues. One of which is skill development. Often, I write content related to specific skill development in one or more areas of life. This is where insufficient training, lack of information, and inadequate skill development can foster, for most, a lack of confidence, clarity, and comprehension of the process. I have seen this way too often over the years. Individuals with great potential, tremendous desire, and ambition fall short of accomplishments they seek because they lack the effective technical and tactical training, support, coaching, or leadership to succeed. I have also discovered that even when these individuals are adequately trained and equipped with skills, knowledge, and competence, they still do not perform at peak levels. They seem to struggle in gaining the consistent results which produce momentum. They have what it takes to win big in their pursuits yet find themselves held back, experiencing starts and stops, or simply quitting.

For a few years, I found this to be a mystery and questioned the individual's real intent or commitment. How could someone well-trained with access to resources and support claim that they are serious about success yet perform far below their potential? I came to the stark realization that something else beyond training, coaching, or more skill development was at play. There was a struggle happening beneath the surface, creating a less than ideal environment to successfully administer all of the new skills learned, pursue goals with unrelenting vigor, and most importantly, sustain focus. This area was overlooked and underplayed. While the superficial was catered to, there was another area in need of significant attention. It became apparent that other struggles or battles were happening that were the culprit to an eager individual's quest for success that were disrupting. It also became evident to me that these battles were happening deep inside the mind and creating havoc.

As I began to dive deeper into this awareness, I found that not only do we all face invisible enemies, but that I had been in battles with them myself. The longer I studied this common human phenomenon, the more I became convinced that this is where most ambitious, driven, goal-oriented people struggle and often fail in the battle with invisible enemies. This is why I wrote this book; to help you address your battles with invisible enemies and create an effective defense system against future attacks.

These invisible enemies I refer to are not physical or spiritual; however, they affect your physical, spiritual, and emotional well-being. They can hold you hostage in your mind, thereby rendering you completely ineffective or impotent in achieving your goals and dreams. These invisible enemies understand that your mind can be your greatest ally or most fearsome enemy. They understand the connection between thought, emotion, and action. I know that it can seem overwhelming and daunting when you consider what you are up against, quite frankly daily, but you can have victory. The truth is that the more driven you are to make and see positive change, the more you become the target for attacks. Sadly, that is just the way it is, my friends. You will not experience many battles if you are not pursuing much with your gifts and talents. However, the second you take the initiative to seek better living or enact positive change and success, you will experience a greater degree of intensive and frequent attacks from invisible enemies.

Again, take heed! I have written this book for you. We will dive into the many aspects of battling invisible enemies so that once your read is over, you will be able to define them, understand their objectives, identify them and their tactics, create your own I.E.D.S. (Invisible Enemy Defense System), establish your tactics for battle, and recognize the blessing that comes from the battle.

Now, if you're ready, SUIT UP and get BATTLE READY!

"YOUR GREATEST BATTLES ARE NEVER EXTERNAL...

...THEY'RE INTERNAL."

DOUBT
DISCOURAGEMENT
ANXIETY
DISAPPOINTMENT
FEAR HOPELESS
SADNESS

CHAPTER ONE

DEFINING INVISIBLE ENEMIES

"When You Discover Your Purpose, Your Enemies Devise a Plot"

In Webster's dictionary, the definition of enemy reads "someone who hates another; someone who attacks or tries to harm another; something that harms or threatens someone or something." This standard definition of enemy is quite suitable when we speak of the traditional understanding of an enemy. However, when defining invisible enemies, the traditional definition does not hold up simply because the attack, threat, or harm propagated is not from a conventional enemy. Even though an invisible enemy intends to harm you or thwart your progress to a significant degree, the tactics are incredibly different. Examining this further is well worth doing if you are going to be victorious in battle. Consider this. You battle an enemy that you cannot see, touch, hear, smell, nor sense. There are no warning signs. They do not fight fair, and their attacks are subtle. You ask how can you possibly battle with such an enemy and expect to win, right? This is why so many are facing inner struggles to their detriment and are not advancing in their worthy pursuits. Can you see the challenge that the uninformed or ill-equipped face when they do not adequately define their invisible adversaries? So, let's understand what invisible enemies are.

Invisible enemies are your own antagonistic and contradictory thoughts, feelings, emotions, and inner chatter that do not align with the image that you hold of yourself. The reason why they are antagonistic and contradictory is because they are not congruent with your identity. That being said (and as an essential subject to discuss at another time), it is worth noting that you should have a positive and healthy identity. If you do not, then your invisible enemies will only continue to provide you "evidence" supporting your negative and unhealthy view of yourself. These do not come in the form of negative and contradictory thoughts, emotions, or inner chatter, but more as approving ones to keep you from changing the identity you hold of yourself. Does this make sense to you? In other words, why allow the fixing of something that is already broken? If you are in a bad place, then the goal is to keep you there. However, for those with a personal identity that is quite firm, healthy, clear, though still under construction, the best way to derail you from your purpose is to begin to stir a sense of dissonance or discord with how you see yourself. This is achieved by introducing a series of coordinated yet subtle attacks that can bring you to your emotional, economic, and achievement knees, reducing you to a pile of wasteful mush. These crafty enemies know that they have created a foothold for advancement if they can affect your thoughts.

If there is one unique thing about human beings, it's that we have, for better or for worse, very active imaginations. So, it only takes a thought or two, and we are off to the races creating a full-length feature mental

film. Isn't it true? Of course, it is. It doesn't take much for us to drift off into Neverland. Whether positive or negative, one strong thought that captures your attention and imagination can hold you hostage, illicit a strong emotion, or steer your next decision.
In most cases, when that thought is left unchecked, all three can occur and produce something incredibly valuable or downright disastrous. Has that ever happened to you? I'm sure it has.

When speaking of hostile or incompatible feelings to the image you hold of yourself, I want you to recall times when you felt overwhelmed, incompetent, unworthy, weak, stressed out, or anxious. The onset and duration of these irrational feelings did not serve to promote your identity and self-image. They did the exact opposite. They stifled and even produced confusion. Can a person struggling with feelings that challenge their self-image create, let alone sustain any positive momentum towards their goals and dreams? Hardly. Therefore, the unsuspecting manipulation of irrational feelings can be a powerful attack if you ignore how you feel and allow an unproductive thought to run amuck in your being. To state that negative emotions play a significant role in your battles is an understatement. We are all emotional beings. Strong emotions drive our actions and decisions. These emotions become the rudders that play a significant role in navigating how and when we arrive at our destiny. So, it's an excellent place for invisible enemies to forge an attack. The reality is that the greater your dream, then the greater your drive and desires are. The nobler your purpose is, the greater the probability that you are more emotionally consumed than most. The clearer your plan is, the more emotionally entrenched you are to see it through. What a wonderful arrangement for an attack. Can you see it? I hope so.

Finally, the worst one of all, the habitual negative inner chatter...the inner voices of doom. Have any of you ever experienced such "delightful" moments when you are visited by the internal chatter of everything adverse to your dreams, identity, and noble attempts? Don't these unsolicited visits suck? Yes, they do. Here you are, minding your own business, then all of a sudden, your inner chatter starts badgering, tempting, and taunting you. It plants the seed of Doubt. This unsolicited, internal monologue can cast dark impressions in your mind as well. They sound something like this:

"What makes you think that this is going to work?"
"This is just who you are."
"Face the facts, you suck!"
"This is going to take too long."
"You realize that not too many ever succeed at this, right?"
"Here you go again. You're not cut out for this."
"You'll never catch up."
"You're broke and busted."
"You're not talented enough."
"Your life is a mess."
"People like you never achieve much."

…and so on. Can you relate? I mean, it seems like your feet haven't hit the ground yet when you wake up in the morning, and the chatter picks up where it left off the night before. The verbal gunfire resumes the minute your eyes open. Am I talking to anybody right now? The dream-stealing and spirit-crushing inner chatter serves only to add insult to injury and rounds out the rest of the coordinated thoughts and emotions that reveal what you must know about invisible enemies and their objectives.

CHAPTER TWO

KNOW YOUR ENEMIES' OBJECTIVES

There is an understanding of who your enemy is and their ultimate objectives in any military engagement or tactical defense planning. In this manner, an effective offensive or defensive campaign can be designed and implemented. This is no different than when battling your invisible enemies. Not only must you identify what they are, but you must be aware of their intentions if you stand to be victorious in battle. In every historical battle known to humanity, where an enemy attacked a group or country, that enemy had a predetermined goal. The attack was not random nor executed without precise planning. The objectives were clear from the beginning so that the potential for failure would be minimized. Such is the case with our inner struggles with mental adversaries. I contend that their clear objectives are to **harass, enslave, torment, and coerce** you. These are very potent and damaging objectives that you must be mindful of and not take lightly. The fact is that when you are under any of these influences, you cannot be productive, let alone perform at your peak, can you? You become absorbed contending with each, if not all, of these enemy-contrived objectives. Let's briefly examine how each objective can take its toll on your focus, joy, and energy.

When an invisible enemy harasses you, you are continually reminded of your mistakes and failures. The negative thoughts of failure, scarcity, inferiority, awkwardness, self-judgment, and condemnation just keep coming in one form or another. It truly is mental, emotional, and spiritual harassment of the worst kind because it comes from within. It can be relentless. How effective can you possibly be at any task when you are under such bombardment? How can you boldly attempt something new or try to improve in one area or another under this condition? The answer is that you can't. The objective of **enslavement** is to keep you so focused on your **fears, worries, and concerns** that you completely shut down and cower in the corner. You became enslaved to your thoughts, irrational feeling, and habitual inner chatter. When you are enslaved in such a way, you cannot do much for yourself, let alone anyone else. This type of enslavement forces you to disengage from the rest of the world and retreat to a place of isolation. Isolated people rarely contribute to society. Mentally, emotionally, and spiritually enslaved people rarely share their gifts and talents with the world, which is a potent objective for an invisible enemy. When an invisible enemy is tormenting you, you never feel right about your life, abilities, or outcome. It seems that no matter what you attempt to do, think, or feel, you can't seem to shake this feeling of idleness or uselessness. There is a nagging that something is missing or that you can do more. You struggle to feel a sense of accomplishment or fulfillment. You struggle with self-blame. You are not convinced yet of your worth, and it torments you. The result here is that afflicted people never find the inner peace needed or personal forgiveness for some past mistake to generate consistent progress towards their goals and dreams.

Finally, when you are being choked by more than you can handle, and the pressure has mounted to a level that you cannot bear, you become vulnerable to **coercion**. In other words, you end up making a decision that you know you never would have made under different circumstances. Can you recall a past decision you made that you now regret but made based on what you were thinking, feeling, or going through at that moment? How did that decision work out for you? Probably not very well. More than likely, it set you back further or threw you so off course that it took you time to recover. My guess is, that decision caused you to experience discouragement, despair, and possibly depression...all results that drew you further away from your destiny. Now that we have investigated what invisible enemies and their objectives are, it is critical to understand why they are personally dangerous to you.

You might be thinking at this point that these battles with invisible enemies, while problematic and undoubtedly harmful to your emotional, psychological, and spiritual well-being, are part of life. You may even go as far as wondering what all the fuss is about. After all, everyone faces inner struggles often, don't they? Your coping method may be to sweep the battles under the rug and chalk it up to life. Well, you would be making a grave mistake. One that falls right into the hands of invisible enemy tactics, which disregard and dismiss them as something that comes and goes without much scarring. It would behoove you to know why these adversaries are so personally dangerous to you. They are harmful to any determined person who strives for better, for more, for positive change, fulfillment, meaningful contribution, and happiness. I submit to you that invisible enemies only serve to destroy, divert, and distract you from your destiny. They serve no other purpose. There is no alternate plan. If, through their tactics, you never reach your greatest potential or stop trying, then for them, it is mission accomplished.

If you're honest, you'll admit that it is during those moments that you are close to your most remarkable breakthrough or milestone that you experience your most difficult inner struggle. It is as if all harmful components have aligned to make you miserable right before your breakthrough. You can't put your finger on it, but you know that something isn't right. We've all been there.

Well, my friends, comprehend that when your purpose is in sync with a well thought out plan, your invisible enemies will devise a plot. This plot is to entangle you with doubt, disbelief, or discouragement (to name a few) so that you lose focus or hope and never reach your destiny. The fact is that your dream is worth fighting for, and you can't succumb to defeat simply because the battles become too intense for you to ignore them. If you are willing and able to continue in the fight, the next step is to know your enemy by name.

CHAPTER THREE

WHEN ATTACKS OCCUR

There is an advantage that exists to know when attacks are more than likely to occur. This knowledge can either prepare you for the potential onslaught, shield you from any attempt, or ward off the attack. When I was not paying attention to my circumstances or mental surroundings, I am attacked the fiercest. I can recall when I had just been interviewed on a popular radio show, and it had gone exceptionally well. The listening audience was providing excellent feedback that I had knocked it out of the park. Yet as I sat there, in an instant, I went from feeling like a champ to feeling like a chump. A subtle but coordinated attack from Despair and Discouragement's invisible enemies robbed me of the joy that I felt just seconds earlier. No one noticed, but my head dipped down into my chin, and my shoulders slumped forward. To a trained eye, they would have seen by reading my body language that I was experiencing something right there and then. However, through a recovery technique that I have learned (which we will discuss in the next chapter), I handled that attack and recovered with only "minor bruises." I did not realize how vulnerable I was to an attack at that moment. I did not take inventory of the situation and consider how an invisible enemy could use it as an opportunity to strike. As such, you must become mindful of when enemy attacks have the most remarkable propensity to stage an offense against you. I submit to you that the following examples are situations of such a time.

1. When you are most vulnerable is often a convenient time for an assault— being vulnerable means that you have allowed yourself to slack on your defense system or have created the perfect scenario for an enemy visit. Let me share with you a couple of examples to illustrate this point.

Recently, I attended a major company convention. On the way back from the evening awards ceremony, I shared a cab ride with an attendee, Jacob, who seemed pretty gloomy. I found that strange, considering that the awards ceremony was fascinating, inspiring, and motivating. His body language, facial expressions, and tone gave his thoughts away. When I asked him what he thought of the evening's event, he responded that it was okay. Jacob went on to say that he was not sure if the business was the right fit for him any longer. After prying a little further, he confessed that he was discouraged because he thought that he would indeed be recognized for at least some achievement. It was painful to be reminded of how much he hasn't accomplished after so much effort. You could see Discouragement dripping from him. This brother was under attack—no question about it. I knew there and then that, unbeknownst to him, he had created the fertile ground for a barrage of offenses. He walked into that convention event entirely and utterly vulnerable to attack. Can you see that? Jacob set himself up with unrealistic expectations or too high expectations. He also began to compare his success against others who had experienced more success than he had. What a vulnerable place for an attack!

Janet was very intent on getting in shape by the summer. Her goal was to fit into a smaller bathing suit and get some of her groove back. It was essential to look good again because her confidence and self-esteem were at stake. Also, she felt that her husband's eye was starting to wander. In March, she joined a gym, cut out pictures of women with similar figures that she was aiming for, and even went out and bought the bathing suits in the sizes she wanted to be in. Now, on the surface, this is perfectly fine to do. I applauded it when she told me about it (she had asked me for fitness advice since she knew that I was a prior fitness trainer). However, I thought to myself, "I hope she isn't setting herself up for an attack." Her time frame seemed a bit unrealistic, not to mention, her purpose for taking such action was more than just health reasons. There was a lot more going on there. Can you see that? I ran into her a few months later, and she looked somewhat the same. I didn't notice any significant weight loss or physical change. When I asked her how it went, her response was, "It was silly to think that I could have changed anything so soon," and "some things just take time." I got the sense that there was more to that answer than I'll ever need to know. Nonetheless, could you say that she experienced (and may still be experiencing) battles? Without question.

Apart from these examples, becoming vulnerable to an attack can also include when you are sick, under the influence of alcohol or drugs, physically tired, frustrated, lonely, overworked, in mourning, and even at certain times of the day. I know that my most vulnerable time of the day, when I need to be aware of possible attacks, is in the morning. This is usually when your mind is still adjusting to the realities of being awake and is highly receptive and suggestive. When you make the crossover from mostly unconscious to conscious, you are incredibly wide open to mental and spiritual aggression. It only takes a second to plant a thought, present an image, or receive a silent utter during this vulnerable time, and it hits you like a torpedo. The result can be felt throughout the day. Bottom line...your vulnerability must be guarded.

2. When you are likely to experience the nastiness of an invisible enemy, the second occasion is when your defenses are down. You are responsible for equipping yourself with the necessary protection to ward off offenses.

That is your job. If you do not handle this, then who will? So, take responsibility here and begin to work towards reinforcing your personal growth and development. Commit to working on you. I find that those who have the biggest and most drawn-out battles invest very little time, money, and energy in self-improvement and empowerment. They are the ones that do not read enough or at all, don't attend workshops or seminars, don't hear good content, or neglect being around people that can build them up. Any shortage of these intellectual, mental, emotional, and spiritual strength-building activities can only further cripple you and your defenses, making you easy prey.

3. You will find that another opening for an attack to take place is when you are distracted by goals, gimmicks, and goblins. Let me explain this further.

Goals are great things and an invaluable aspect to your motivation, focus, and performance. They serve as a measure to which you can monitor your progress and achievements. However, when you become so absorbed with the attainment of the goals to the point that you begin to lose touch with your environment, relationships, health, and others' needs, you are in line for a nasty attack. The pursuit of a worthwhile goal is noble and honorable but not at the expense of losing yourself. The challenge with high achievers, entrepreneurs, peak performance individuals, dreamers, and just about anybody with a decent measure of ambition is that we can get so caught up with the thrill of accomplishment that we become numb to everything else. Am I speaking to anyone right now? If you're reading this book, then you're probably relating to this extremely well, aren't you? Well, then you can be heading towards, or have already been blindsided by, an invisible enemy simply because you weren't paying attention. By the way, blindsided attacks are the worst because they take longer to recover from. Being distracted by gimmicks is nothing more than chasing the next ample opportunity or deal. I have met many great people who gave up everything (or just about) to pursue a new business, investment, or venture for the promise of wealth or incredible financial gain. These individuals were convinced that this gimmick was their ticket to ride that common sense and counsel were unappreciated and disregarded. What an attack in the making! Sure enough, things have not gone well for those that I have spoken within this situation. The hardest battle they are dealing with right now is not the loss of money, valuables, or pride but the gain of shame, guilt, distrust, and knowing that they have let others down. This is a tough place, and anyone going through this right now would undoubtedly agree. Chasing gimmicks can prove to be an unfortunate opportunity for an attack.

Next comes the potential for battle with an invisible enemy when you are distracted by goblins. What do I mean by goblins? I mean any person, group, company, or even ideology who makes promises or sells you a dream that leads you astray. Goblins cannot be trusted because they can present what is worthless as worthy, and they often convince you to compromise your beliefs or standards. When you buy into their phony promises or pledges and abandon all common sense to the point of social isolation, you have just constructed an ideal condition for an attack. Many have succumbed to a nasty battle because goblins wooed them.

4. Finally, I am convinced that your enemy looks for favorable circumstances to stage a blitz and find it unguarded when you have left the front door. In other words, no one is standing guard at the doorway of your mind. Your mental sentinel has either not been called to duty or is out on sick leave. Either way, you have no protection for the most important

treasure that exists for you...your mind. Let me share this thought with you.

Imagine leaving your house or apartment every day to head off to work and never close your front door. In fact, not only do you not lock it, but you leave it wide open with all of your expensive valuables exposed for anyone driving or walking by to see. To make matters worse, you have no alarm system whatsoever. You live in a neighborhood with known convicted burglars as your neighbors. Now, that sounds pretty outrageous, and no one would ever conceive of doing such a thing, right? Well, that's exactly what most do. They leave their mind wide open for any sorts of attacks and ransacking to happen. With the same diligence that you would shut the front door, lock it, turn on the alarm system, and even get a big dog to guard your stuff, you must do the same to defend the entry point to your mind. Are you getting this? By the way, this is done by intention every single day. If you do not purposely place a mental guard at the doorway, it will not appear independently. Choosing every day to protect the most critical asset you have is tantamount to avoiding or warding off unnecessary skirmishes that will only serve to distract you and zap you of your energy. Left unguarded, your mind will be susceptible to the whims of an invisible enemy.

NOTE: For the following chapters, we will use IE as a stand-in for "Invisible Enemy."

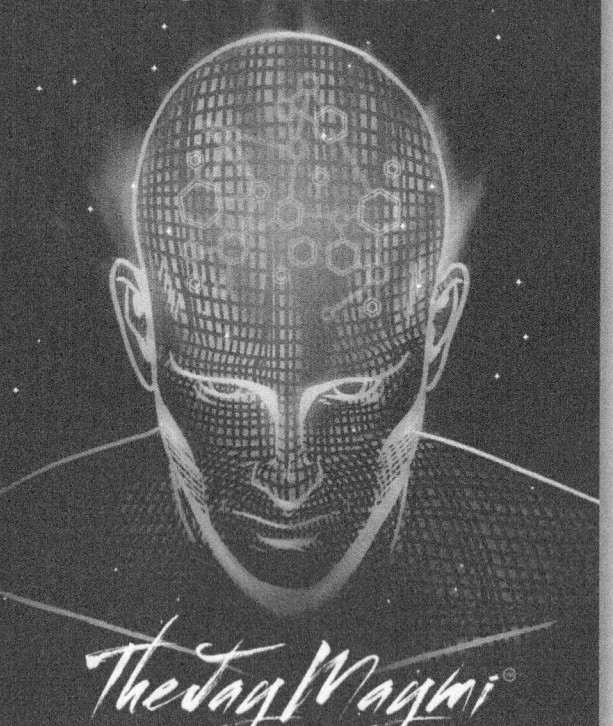

CHAPTER FOUR

THE DOWNWARD SPIRAL MODEL OF INVISIBLE ENEMY ATTACKS

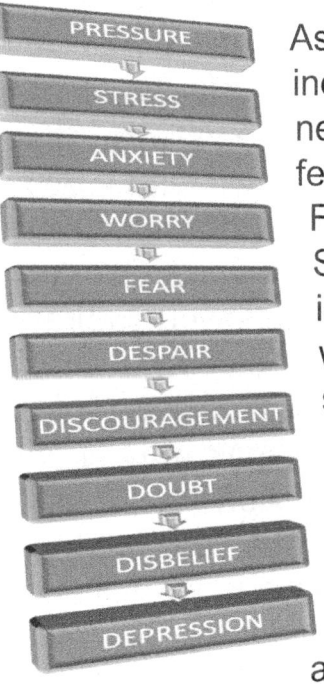

As we dive into this incredibly enlightening next section, there are a few things to take note of. First, the Downward Spiral Model of IE attacks is something I came up with after carefully studying the common attacks that many have experienced (including yours truly). I noticed a pattern of inner struggle that seemed almost coordinated. As I examined my battles and began interviewing others, I found that there did exist a pattern to these attacks and that no one attack was by chance. As you read through this next section and understand the different IE attacks in this model, you will also observe the same attack patterns in your life. This is good news, my friends, because the better you can understand the warfare that you and I are in, the better equipped we become for battle and hence, victory.

Secondly, although the model shows a progression of attacks, it does not necessarily mean that you will experience every episode. There have been times when you may encounter one or two, and it ends there, or you may experience a number of them, seemingly at the same time. Consider this an IE barrage. However, if you embrace this model, you will find that one attack typically leads to another. You hardly find yourself struggling with despair without first struggling with Worry or Anxiety. You will see what I mean as you continue your read. It's also worth knowing that this model's stages or attacks can happen quickly or take years to develop. Remember that IE can be very patient in delivering their blows. You may be in a stage of battle that has strapped you in for a few years now. The key is to recognize the attack and see your way out before the next one aims.

Finally, you will see that there are two phases to this model. This is because I firmly believe that two phases do exist in creating a difficult scenario for you to escape from ultimately. *Phase I* is intended to take early shots so that you become distracted, dazed, drained of energy, and focus while weakening you physically, emotionally, and spiritually. This sets up *Phase II,* which introduces the weightier attacks designed to finish the job.

IMPORTANT NOTE:
Before we get started, I must mention that you have to be aware that there is a difference between an invisible enemy attack and a justifiable feeling. Not every justifiable feeling is an attack, and, indeed, not every attack is a justifiable feeling. Let me clarify. Suppose your next big promotion is not given to you or you missed it by a little. In that case, a feeling of disappointment is justifiable, and it is not an attack. If your significant other breaks up with you, then feeling hurt and momentarily depressed is a justifiable

emotion. It is not an attack. If you have a car that is close to being repossessed, and you're worried because the next payment is due and you're short on the money, well, that is a justifiable feeling and not an attack of worry. Contrarily, high anxiety is not a justifiable feeling. Deep-seated doubt is not a justifiable feeling. These differences will become more apparent and evident as you continue your read.

PHASE I – THE SETUP

PRESSURE

Did you know that over 40 songs are written to date with the word PRESSURE in the title? Famous singer Billy Joel's hit song "Pressure" ranks as the most popular. Even as I write this book, one of the popular songs being played is "Rescue Me" from Thirty Seconds to Mars. It speaks of being rescued from "the demons in my mind." Pressure and its repercussions are such a common human experience that it captures themes in music. People find this topic so relatable that songs written about it appeal to the vast majority of the population. When thinking about times you've been operating under burdensome duress, it is easy to see how your performance, attitude, and creative ability can be affected. This first IE attack becomes the perfect set up for the Downward Spiral's first wave in the Downward Spiral Model. This IE knows all too well the effectiveness of pressure in the lives of those seeking more out of life. This first enemy starts the battle with an initial attack of pressure. In my experience, pressure is the result of being overwhelmed or burdened by several factors. One of these factors is promises made. The minute you make a promise to someone, you have the pressure to come through with it.

There is nothing wrong with making a promise if you know that it is rational and reasonable to keep. However, if you already suspect that the commitment you just made may be out of your reach, then you've newly created an opportunity for the IE of Pressure to strike. When you set unrealistic goals, you can find yourself feeling the pressure of trying to attain them. When you are struggling financially, and bills are due, pressure decides to sit down with you and have coffee. It could be the pressure to right a wrong you've done or the daily grind to be a role model to your colleagues, family, and the public in general, even the desire to get to the gym for your health's sake. These, and so many more, become opportunities for an attack. The bottom line is the more you take on, the greater the probability for an attack. Since pressure becomes so easy to apply and can be incredibly useful and damaging, it plays a significant role in the spiral's commencement. The most effective way to eliminate the threat of an attack of pressure is to say "NO" more often. Saying "no" or "not now" when presented with yet something else to commit to is wise and serves to protect you from an unnecessary attack. Don't take too much on. Don't make goals that you will struggle to attain. Stop promising everything to everybody. The invisible enemy of pressure can't attack you if you give it nothing to work with. Make sense?

STRESS

When pressure has taken a solid hold of you, the next attack is one of Stress. Stress can develop from prolonged and unfettered pressure. When you wake up every day to the same pressures and have not found relief of any kind, then the attack of stress begins. This IE starts to aim the attack at you physically and emotionally. We all know that stress is one of the leading causes of health degradation. Severe or chronic stress is physically dangerous because it can interfere with your ability to live an everyday life, not to mention elevate the hormone cortisol to hazardous levels. In the emotional sense, you can become increasingly irritable and impatient with others rendering you not a nice person to be around, which only exacerbates the situation. Pressure and Stress are the IE's favorite 1 - 2 punch.

ANXIETY

After stress has done its job, it is up to the enemy of Anxiety to enter and shoot at you. Pressure and stress pave the way for anxiety to begin rearing its ugly head. Stress can take its toll on you physically; heightened anxiety will often result in outside chemical substances needed to bring you under control or a manageable state.

I have always seen anxiety as the ongoing, nonstop chatter and imagery in your mind. In other words, when your mind keeps going even after you desire it to slow down or change direction, you are experiencing a measure of Anxiety. It will also force your heart to race and feel physically "off" as well. For some, this is where taking prescriptions become a remedy for anxiety. Although I am not advocating one way or another for the usage of medications to deal with Anxiety, I do recognize that it can be a necessity for many. How you handle Anxiety is not what this section is about. Understanding how you can encounter the IE of Anxiety is. Incidentally, Anxiety is the increase of Pressure and Stress. The IE of Anxiety says figuratively, "let's turn up the heat a little." I told you they don't fight fair, didn't I? The bigger concern is that when you have to resort to outside chemical substances to regulate you internally, it can slightly rob you of your power, confidence and introduce a sense of loss of control. All of this continues to affect your ability to perform at peak levels with sustained, concentrated effort. People facing a battle with anxiety can be handicapped on their journey to success, which sets up the next attack...Worry.

WORRY

At the level of worry, things begin to get intense because worry can cripple you. When you worry about one or a few things, your energy and focus go to the things you are worried about. Isn't this true? It doesn't matter if the worry stems from your performance, a relationship, a sale, your finances, or the unresolved situations keeping you in bondage. With pressure, stress, and anxiety, or you cannot shake the feeling of the apocalypse coming, this IE has you exactly where it wants you...distracted and dysfunctional. Can you see this?

When worry has taken your thoughts hostage, you end up delaying your dreams. The cleverness in the attack of worry is that it's self-preserving. I mean that the very things we are worrying about only causes us to continue to think about them. Does this make sense? If this IE has you entangled with thoughts of Worry, then no matter how hard you try, your thoughts revert to the things you are worried about, which only keeps you worried. Are you getting this? Thought-entangled people struggle with the mental freedom needed to grab hold of their destiny victoriously.

Let me challenge you on this. Think about something that you are worrying about now. Go ahead. Just take a second and then come back. Now, how hard was it to get away from that thought? How quickly did that thought or issue that has you worried (and anxious) start to take on a greater energy or life than you wanted it to? Can you see how in a few more minutes, it could have ballooned? As a result, your Worrying would have increased. This is truly one of the dastardliest of attacks, and it carries a whopping punch!

FEAR
Rounding out Phase 1 is Fear. Once Pressure, Stress, Anxiety, and Worry have mangled you, the enemy of Fear delivers the

most crippling assault. It is the most emotionally damaging of all of the IE attacks because it completely changes your demeanor in an instant and keeps you there longer than you'd want to be. Fear will have you believe in situations that are not happening. As a follow up to Worry, Fear convinces you that the things you are worried about will come to pass. It has a way of mesmerizing you into buying a lie. Fear is a liar! Fear will rob your joy and turn your days into dread.

I experienced this recently as I was traveling to a speaking engagement in New York. Although I had prepared for the trip, the pressure to perform was a little weighty. Then, Worry stepped in and said, "what if your flight is delayed? You'll miss the event." Of course, the flight was on time. However, that didn't stop Fear from launching its attempt when the thought popped in my mind that the rental car place would not have a car available. After all, the rental car company's site did say that inventory was extremely low. Even though I had already reserved the car online and was guaranteed to have one, I still became scared that there would not be a car available for me. I became so caught up in the lie that I may not have a car that I started to panic and send text messages for people to come pick me up. Isn't that crazy?

Instead of concentrating on my workshop event and focusing on final preparation, I was in panic mode, looking for someone to come pick me up when I already had a car waiting for me, which I had paid for in advance. My excitement and joyful anticipation of a great event quickly turned to pressure, then to worry, then, ultimately, ear. I was counter-punched! The enemy of fear capitalizes on the returns that a little fear can produce. These include irrational thinking, increased health issues, increased anxiety, isolation, a complete shutdown of trust in others, a pause in your dreams, and a change in mood and attitude. The struggle is genuine for those in the heat of this attack. Have you ever been there? I'm sure you have. I would submit to you that the greatest component of this mental cancer is the scars you are left with once you can break free if you ever do.

They become reminders of where you were and markers for return attacks.

You see, if you are prone to fear of failure, then you will be visited by the enemy of Fear once again to attack you in that area. Suppose your struggle with fear has been in the area of acceptance or validation with your peers. In that case, if left unresolved, you will leave a clear marker that can be exploited again at some other point. Additionally, Fear can be the catalyst for irresponsible actions and irrational decisions that can result in devastating chaos. Ultimately, the IE of Fear intends to leave you lost, without direction, and wobbling at the knees of your breakthrough. Exactly where Despair wants you to be.

PHASE II – THE KNOCKOUT

DESPAIR
The IE of Despair has an entirely different plan than any of the prior IE Many who are currently struggling with a sense of despair or have had previous struggles will testify that

despair served only to debilitate their hope. The result of one who has faced this enemy is that they no longer have the same level of hope that they had before. I won't go as far as saying that all hope is lost, but it sure seems like it has taken an extended lunch break. Despair has a way of putting blinders on you so that your vision is limited to only the problems in front of you and not the possible solutions that may exist. Despair's challenge is that you convince yourself that there is no way out or, at minimum, getting out is incredibly difficult. The expectancy of positive change, dreams realized, goals attained, and fulfillment achieved that gave you so much buoyancy has been reduced to rubble, and it hurts. It pains you to know that better exists. Yet, better seems so unreachable. Despair forces you to question your prior decisions. After all, if you had made different decisions, you would be further along your journey to your dreams. No one likes to guess themselves second, but that is precisely what this unseen adversary wants you to do. The attack aims to question your capability and judgment and render you impotent for future ones.

Probably the most vicious aspect of this attack, though, is the sense that you are running out of time. As each day passes and your dreams are still far off, your debts are not diminishing, and you are no better off than you were 5, 3, or even one year ago, despair digs deeper roots. It paves the way for the next major blow of Discouragement.

DISCOURAGEMENT
After 35 years (and counting) as an entrepreneur, author, counselor, coach, and manager, I can say without question that the IE battle that most people have experienced is Discouragement. Although all experience this emotional malady, and no one is immune, it dramatically affects those highly motivated. I have always been persuaded that the greater the dream, the greater the discouragement that awaits. Now, don't get me wrong. I'm not saying that goals should not be pursued because of impending discouragement, nor am I saying that discouragement is the result you find after giving your all to your efforts. I am merely stating that discouragement will be an inevitable attack because of your desires'

greater intensity. As your desires increase, so will the intensity of the attack. Having access to this insight allows you to cope with the attack in a way that will not derail you entirely from your goals. It does for many who give up because discouragement's pain and discomfort is too much to bear. It is important to understand what gives rise to Discouragement and how this IE waits for the right time to attack. When you experience despair, disappointment, and delay, you can expect an attack from this enemy. Since we have already dissected Despair, let's focus on Disappointment and Delay in greater detail.

Disappointment can be felt when you are let down by a less than favorable result. People can let you down. Companies can let you down. You can let yourself down. All of these variables that can let you down breed disappointment. The challenge is that one disappointment after another creates an explosive effect that becomes harder to bounce back from. Why do people quit something that they were so excited about initially? It's simple. After so many unrealized expectations, unfulfilled promises, lackluster results, violated trust, poor support, and so on, they become so disappointed that to stop the discomfort, it is easier just to quit. The multiple disappointments created one part of Discouragement. The other trigger, and most people have little patience, is the delay in seeing their efforts produce the desired results.

Even in most worthwhile pursuits, there is always a delay for some reason or another. Discouragement can start to take root when results begin to take too long. This is where patience comes into play and must be exercised. The hidden adversary wants nothing more than to get you so discouraged that you slow down tremendously. Discouraged people tend to slow down because little they see for their efforts, so why bother to go hard. Has that ever happened to you? You wanted something so wrong and gave it all you had to achieve it, but it was just not happening fast enough. All you kept experiencing was disappointment and delay. As a result, you reduced the amount of energy, attention, money, and time you put in before. Why? You became discouraged. When you have been battling discouragement for some time, you begin to struggle with Doubt.

DOUBT

In the Downward Spiral Model of invisible enemy attacks, doubt is hazardous. If discouragement leads you to slow down your progress, doubt forces you to hit the pause button. When you are in the throes of doubt, it infiltrates many aspects of your beliefs. In other words, you begin to doubt if you're good enough for the prize you seek. You question if your talents and skills are adequate for the task. You lack the confidence to continue the path you started. A deepened degree of doubt can go past you and extend itself to doubting the people around you, your company, and the process. You doubt that you will ever achieve the life you desire. You doubt you can change yourself or the things around you. The scary thing is that even when you are given reason not to doubt and have been presented with enough evidence to renew your faith and give life to your convictions, you still stay saddled with doubt. Doubt also begins to cause you to either stray from your intended path or consider a new one altogether. Here is the tragedy in that. You were given a dream and an assignment that stirs your soul when you think about it. Your gifts and talents were purposely forged in you for a greater destiny. This is why you are so determined, hungry, and a badass. No one else can do what you were tasked to do, so when doubt takes you for a ride, you lose sight of who you are and what you were meant to do. This is why I mentioned earlier that this is one of the most dangerous attacks. When the enemy of Doubt has got you in its grasp, you can no longer muster enough enthusiasm to stay in that pursuit for very much longer. As the previous attacks began to drain your faith slowly, Doubt makes sure that the tank is near empty. A Doubtful person is in limbo and has been sidelined for the time being. Now, can a Doubtful person return to a place of reinvigorated faith again? Yes. Absolutely. However, the uphill climb will be steep and arduous, and many lack the will to see it through, further pulling you down the spiral.

DISBELIEF

The jump from Doubting to Disbelieving is but a short distance away. This is why the IE of Doubt and Disbelief can appear to be one. However, they are the final 1-2 punch combination before the worst IE of them all arrives. The challenge with Disbelief is that you have abandoned ship on believing in yourself, your dreams, and your abilities. Whereas belief can still be resurrected when your struggling with Doubt, there is no chance when you are in full-blown Disbelief. The end game of a struggle with Disbelief is to completely hit the stop button on the journey you were on. The fruit you were going to bear now has a great probability that no one will ever experience it.

Disbelief robs the world of the good you could have brought it when your mission or desires were accomplished. How many have died and their dreams right along with them? Why? One reason (which I believe firmly in because I have seen it) is that they could not shake the shroud of Disbelief that they lived with. Regardless of how many attempts they made to rebuild their belief in their hopes and dreams again, they could not muster enough thrust to restart believing. Incidentally, those who are more prone to attacks from this IE tend to have challenges with their belief systems already. In other words, there is a dysfunctional undercurrent of belief that is quietly running beneath the surface of their conscious mind. This only serves to worsen the situation because you are more apt to reject anything aimed at helping you. When you are in the midst of the struggle, it doesn't matter what anyone says because you no longer accept or receive others' encouragement. Quite frankly, you become unreachable in that sense. The danger here is that disbelief has the potential to cross into other areas of your life and affect them. It can migrate. Your disbelief may initially be contained to some area of success or world-class achievement that you were pursuing. As a result of the struggle, it affects your identity as a parent, a ministry personnel, a spouse, an entrepreneur, or even an employee.

The bottom line is that this mental, emotional, and spiritual battle can leave you at the worst place you can be asking yourself the question, "Why bother?" The pinnacle of disbelief is when you begin to ask this question. "Why bother...staying in this relationship, going to the gym, talking to more people, studying harder, getting excited, dreaming, reading my affirmations, pumping myself up, planning for the future, saving money, trying, getting better, and so on. It reflects someone who has convinced themselves that things will not change no matter what they do. Finding yourself in this place is quite possibly the most challenging place you can be. If you no longer believe in yourself, your potential, and your future outcome, then who else will? It can become depressing.

DEPRESSION

For this final section, I want to state my position and perspective on this sensitive topic clearly. There are times when Depression requires professional help and medication when dealing with mild to severe depression. These clinically diagnosed individuals should pursue the treatments that are recommended by health care professionals. I completely encourage anyone struggling with deep depression that is clinical to seek the professional help they need.

The Downward Spiral Model of invisible enemy attacks with Depression sheds light on an emotional, mental, and spiritual condition that many driven individuals can encounter. There are many high achievers that, like me, that can be in the struggle with this enemy without ever being diagnosed with depression disorder. They arrive at this place organically through the experiences or encounters with a few or all of the previously discussed IE attacks. I hope I have stated that well.

Nonetheless, arriving at the toughest battle of them all from a go-getter's standpoint is cause for great concern. This attack has the propensity to cause you to withdraw either temporarily or completely from any activity that would remind you of your dream because the pain and hurt is something you don't care for. What pain? The pain of Disbelief, Doubt, Discouragement, Despair,

Fear, Worry, Anxiety, Stress, and Pressure. The onslaught of attacks has made you so weary in battle that you retreat to a place of total idleness and isolation. This battle extracts a heavy toll because it truly renders you unwilling or unable to continue pursuing your dreams. You may even experience a loss of interest in that dream. Sadly, the shutdown you experience due to being depressed, and your awareness of it only feeds your depression further. This can complicate matters because now guilt is introduced. When depression has begun to work its way in your life, you struggle to find inner peace and joy. You may function well and not necessarily, experience the more considerable symptoms of major depression, but you certainly feel less than. I have experienced brief times when I became depressed for all the same reasons every dreamer does. I was surprised to know that many of my clients, achieving friends, business partners, and industry colleagues, shared the same struggle. It was good to feel that I was not alone in these IE attacks. Knowing that others shared the same battles brought me strength and renewed hope.

Eventually, I (as well as they) snapped out of it and became only the stronger and the wiser. So, in the end, what the enemy meant for damage and destruction has been turned around for good. The same will happen for you. Let me encourage you to press on while in this battle. You are not alone. Relief and restoration will come!

CHAPTER FIVE

DEVELOPING YOUR I.E.D.S.
(Invisible Enemy Defense System)

"The best way to win the battle is not get into the battle."

As we turn the corner on our understanding of battling invisible enemies, let's begin to focus on implementing strategies and tactics that defend and/or deflect attacks. I have always believed that the best way to win a fight is to avoid one altogether. All three of my children have been students of Martial Arts. Although not from the same school or style of Martial Arts, each instructor has been consistent in their underlying teachings. They have all taught that the use of Martial Arts is the last resort and avoiding its use is the best defense. In other words, do everything else you can first before engaging in the actual fight. This is the real victory.

However, knowing that you are well equipped and trained to handle the aggression (should all else fail) builds confidence. This same philosophy applies here as well. The best way to win the battles with IE is just not to get into one. Why? It's simple. Too many battles over a consistent period will cripple anyone regardless of who they are. There are times when you and I have faced inner struggles that have taken their toll emotionally, spiritually, mentally, and on occasion, physically. Isn't that true? I mean, it took you a while to get back on your proverbial feet, right? Well, taking on battle after battle like that will only serve to weaken you to the point that you become ineffective, unproductive, and quite possibly, not a nice person to be around. Have you ever met people like this? I'm sure you have. Well, how do you think they got there? They certainly weren't born that way. A series of ugly experiences, nasty internal battles, unresolved struggles, and unchecked thinking brought them to the place they are now. You can avoid a scenario like this by establishing your own I.E.D.S. (Invisible Enemy Defense System). This tactical defense system will help you avoid the battles or quickly get out of them without much harm. Your I.E.D.S. must have 6 Components. The sixth being the most important, as you will see. Let's dive right into it, warriors!

I.E.D.S. COMPONENTS

1. You must know when **YOU** are most vulnerable. As we observed earlier, you are most susceptible to an attack when you are vulnerable. However, just knowing this is not good enough. You must know when YOU are most vulnerable. It takes understanding or realizing the times when, *in your own life*, you are weakest or sensitive, thereby enabling an IE to make a move towards you. Once you have identified these times, you can take caution and be mindful of impending attacks. Being aware of your most vulnerable moments reduces an attack's potency because you are not caught off guard.

2. It would be best if you recognized which enemy it is. As you have read, there are ten enemies that I have detailed; however, identifying which

enemy is launching an offensive is vital for you to battle effectively. For example, the enemy of Fear draws upon different tactics from the enemy of Discouragement. The sooner you're able to detect which enemy is forging an attack, the sooner you can begin your defense. Also, be aware that you can experience multiple enemies at one time as well. Therefore, the ability to determine who's involved in the attack will give you the best chance at victory.

3. You must recognize your enemies' tactics. It's been my experience that attacks are identifiable. Since they work so often, why would an IE need to change them? Here's a comparative example that should illustrate this well.

In football, coaches have a set amount of plays from which they call on during the game. If they find that the same play is working because the defense cannot stop it, they continue to run it. They'll run that play all day long. No reason to change it if it's helping them gain yards. What becomes interesting is that, after a while, the other team becomes aware that the offense is taking the same set of actions before the play begins. This is where they start to make the necessary adjustments to stop the offense from gaining anymore yards. In essence, their early recognition of the offense's repetitive tactics allows them to better defend the play. Can you see the correlation here? You must begin to recognize your IE tactics as a sign of an attack coming. What are IE tactics? Disturbing mental images, whispers, an oppressive heaviness, anxiousness, Fear thoughts, irrational and unrealistic scenarios playing out in your mind, to name just a few. The sooner your I.E.D.S. detects these tactics, the sooner you can begin your defense.

4. Give your yesterdays an eviction notice. If you don't hold on to past guilt, shame, failures, condemnation, hurts, and wrongs, your IE has nothing to

remind you of. Empty yourself of anything that an IE can hold over your head or entice you to recall. If you have to forgive someone or yourself, then do it. If you have to let go of something or someone harmful from your past, then do it. If you have to re-do something, then re-do it. If you have to acknowledge your shortcomings, then accept them. If you have to get mentoring or coaching, then get it. If you have a disbelief that has to be dealt with, then deal with it. Give nothing to your IE to utilize in an attack. Don't provide the foothold that becomes the stronghold.

5. Build an army of like-minded support. It is not rocket science to state that your battles are far more challenging to deal with when alone or isolated. So many people go into retreat mode when they are struggling. When they should reach out for encouragement, support, clarity, a fresh perspective, prayer, or even a loving beat down (which does exist), they do not. This happens by

choice or because they have not created that powerful unit of others who can walk or talk them through the battle or avoid one. I can assure you that a fortified you is not what an IE wants to face. You are so much stronger when you surround yourself with a coalition of those in one accord. There is tremendous power in calling someone when you feel the onset of an attack coming. Knowing that a group of people have got your back is incredibly empowering.

6. Have daily inspections. Check in with yourself. Take a few moments throughout your day to see how you're doing. It only takes a moment to hit the pause button and ask yourself how you're doing. This simple tactic keeps you aware of your feelings, thoughts, and chatter. If anything is gnawing at you, you can acknowledge it and begin to get at its root. Any ambitious go-getter will bypass moments of personal reflection because we get so entrenched in the daily grind for

progress that we miss the small, subtle signs that something is not right within, or the issues that must be dealt with keep getting swept under the rug. Well, any excellent defense system has daily checks frequently. This avoids any potential and unsuspecting attacks from occurring because of early detection. Whatever needs to be addressed, no matter how small, gets addressed immediately. You must approach your day with the same discipline and diligence.

7. Develop tactical strategies to thwart or quickly end an attack once it has been launched. Even though you have an I.E.D.S., there will still be attacks. This is inevitable. As I mentioned earlier in this book, enemies are aggressive, opportunistic, subtle, or bold, do not fight fair, and never stop making attempts. So, you will have to deal with them for as long as you live. Hence, the reason why having a handful of techniques at your disposal is critical to your defense system. I have developed

a few methods that have worked for me and others as well. These tactical methods serve to get you out of the battle as quickly as possible and relatively unscathed.

REPLACEMENT

In the life insurance world (depending on which state you live in), when a client takes your recommendation because you have convinced them that your life insurance policy is better for them than the one they currently own, you must justify that to the insurance companies involved as well as state insurance departments. For simple explanation purposes, this is called Replacement. Replacement procedures require you to provide a few reasons why your policy is more suitable than what the client currently has. This is done to protect the client. Well, this tactic can become an excellent one for you when dealing with an IE attack. When an attack comes that challenges you with negative thoughts, irrational feelings, or negative inner chatter, practice a replacement immediately. Find two or more positive thoughts, affirmations, or justifications to replace that attack and then speak them aloud. Say something like this, "I am diligent in all that I do, and my best days are ahead!", or "There is no one worthier than me to achieve this goal and the recognition I receive proves it!", or "My health is the envy of all. People wonder what gives me so much energy!" Are you getting the picture? This works amazingly because it redirects your thoughts and immediately puts a halt to a potential downward spiral.

SNAP CLAP

Anthony Robbins is the guru of changing your physiology and energy in an instant. He often speaks of making a power move that puts you at a peak state. For those of you familiar with his teachings, you will know this. When battling IE attacks, you also have to employ a similar tactic to interrupt an attack's onset with a physical move. This immediate and quick physical move also changes your physiological state instantaneously, enough to help you get a grip on your thoughts or emotions. This is so vital to do because when your mind is taken hostage, you start to spiral out of control with your thoughts quickly; you have to immediately break that momentum with an action that will snap you out of it. This is why I call this technique the snap clap. It is a one-time (or twice) hard clap that you can do anytime you need to snap out of it. It is an unnoticeable action that will not freak anybody out when you do it. The snap clap has helped me many times, and it works as soon as you know there is an attack commencing.

RECALL AND RECITE

Another very effective technique that leads you back to a good place is recalling the good, positive, happy, and victorious times you've had. Likewise, remembering the past achievements, goals attained, progress made, recognition you've earned, bold and brave actions taken, and how far you've come. You can also throw in there what makes you so unique, memorable, and engaging. Recalling these things and reciting them incorporates two potent agents, memory, redirection, and declaration. It is not good enough to recall, but you must also repeat the words. The combination of reminding yourself of your identity, your accomplishments, and who you are, plus reciting them, changes your vibrational state to one that repels invisible enemies. Your verbal affirmation and declaration of the historical evidence proves the amazing person you send the invisible enemies running for cover. DANG! That feels good!

DAILY INTENTIONS
Every day you have a choice. Every day you and I have a choice whom we will serve. You can choose to serve the actions, thoughts, emotions, and inner chatter that suit you, empower you, support your identity, and bring you closer to your goals and dreams, or you can choose to serve the opposite. You may not intentionally choose the opposite, but the opposite will be chosen for you if you choose nothing at all. This is where the problem lies for many who do not have an effective I.E.D.S. The failure to choose your desired intentions means that you have no dominion over where your thoughts, actions, attractions, feelings, and inner chatter will lead you. You will be essentially tossed back and forth by every invisible enemy tactic. As you awaken and intentionally choose the

authoritative act throughout the day, it is an incredible forceful tool towards warding off IE mental assaults.

RUN WITH THE RIGHT CROWD

You've heard that you become the company you keep, right? Or bad company corrupts good character? Not only is this sound teaching for obvious reasons but also when establishing a solid I.E.D.S. Running with the right crowd that will continuously inspire, encourage, and hold you accountable is vital for a defense system. There is a tremendous advantage in associating with those who have faced (or still face) similar battles because of the relatability factor and strength in numbers. Keep in mind that when you are isolated and alone, you are the weakest.

FLICK IT OFF

Learning to let go of energy-sapping and resistance-creating experiences is another useful technique that has to be a component of your I.E.D.S. Therefore, practice the habit of flicking it off. Consider the parallel that exists when you find lint, a piece of food, a dead bug, or a booger on you. Do you examine it? Does it capture your full attention? Do you make plans to preserve it for a later date? Do you share it with your friends? Does it earn the right to be your latest Facebook or Instagram post? Of course not! You flick it off as soon as you realize what it is. True? It has absolutely no value in your life, so why keep it around. Well, you have to be just as quick to flick off anything that attaches to you that has no value in any aspect of your life. If you don't, then you will be giving IE a foothold to exploit.

THE POWER OF PAST TENSE

At times, one of your defensive maneuvers will be to reprogram your wiring. This seems odd, right? In a recent book I wrote *(7 Powerful Techniques for Effective Subconscious Communication)*, I spend considerable time discussing the subconscious mind. In it, I elaborated that the subconscious does not know what is real or not. It takes as absolute truth whatever you speak, think, or feel with intensity. Therefore, reprogramming your mind as a means of defense planning becomes an excellent discipline to develop. Here's how it works.

Convincing your mind that something is in the past conjures up a sense of peace, calmness, and certainty. It develops a strong sense of empowerment and control because you implant in your subconscious mind that this WAS something I dealt with previously but no longer. Consider the following statements:

"I remember when I struggled with stress."
"I remember when I had very little money in the bank." "I remember when I was lonely."
"I remember when I had low self-esteem."
"I remember when my weight was a concern."
"I remember when I was depressed."
"I remember when..."
"I remember when..."
"I remember when..."

This *Past Tense Speech* technique has the unique ability to reprogram your mind so that a despair or disbelief attack has a more challenging time making inroads because your mind no longer sees that as an issue. It would be best if you got this. We give power and energy to things that we currently are either concerned about or struggling with. These struggles are always accompanied by a set of feelings and thoughts, true? Well, what happens when struggles, battles, or nuances that you have been battling with are over and in the past? What kind of feeling or emotion do you experience when you think about that particular struggle knowing that it is behind you? If you're like me, you feel relief, peace, accomplishment, to name a few, right? Well, you can embrace those same feelings even if you haven't seen the manifestation of those struggles, dreams, goals, and desires yet. This is true faith, believing, feeling, and acting as if you already have what you believe for without physical proof. Is this sinking in? Your IE will become toothless the more you master *Past Tense* thinking and speaking.

EXERCISE AND EAT RIGHT

As a one-time Personal Fitness Trainer and competitive athlete, I understand and wholeheartedly believe in the incredible benefits of regular exercising and proper nutrition. Most people know this as well. However, how could consistently working out and eating right be a component of an effective I.E.D.S.? Simple. When you look good, you feel good. When you feel good, you are much more empowered and thereby able to withstand harmful enemy trickery. When you look like crap, and you feel like crap, well, good luck. Your ability to resist will be significantly hindered because you already feel less than, and here comes something else to seriously contend with. Besides that, what stamina do you think you'll have to battle with if you're in a struggle for a prolonged period? Let me encourage you. If you are not currently engaged in a level of exercise and proper nutrition, then begin immediately. You will find that it is a worthwhile effort to pursue.

IN CLOSING

"Within the Battles Lies the Blessing."

No one enjoys struggles of any kind. Whether brief skirmishes or prolonged battles, avoiding or never encountering them would be the desire of most sane people, myself included. If I never experience another IE attack, battle, or inner struggle again, I would be overjoyed. The smile would be from ear to ear. I believe that you echo my sentiments, right? Well, as much as this would be ideal, it is also highly probable not to happen. So, what do you do? You realize that within the battle lies the blessing if you are inclined to find it. In all of my battles, and those who have shared theirs with me, I have found that you can find the silver lining from every inner struggle you face. Let me submit to you that there are four (and probably more) blessings that every battle will reveal.

The first is that you **discover something new about yourself**. That particular struggle with Doubt, Worry, or Anxiety will be quite uncomfortable, annoying, and draining; however, you will realize how strong you can be when you get through it. You also arrive at a higher level of personal confidence that you didn't know existed. Even though the battle may have been fierce, you learn that you are not a quitter, which gives you renewed strength. The fact is that you can only learn something new about yourself, unearth a dormant characteristic, or a long-suppressed and unhandled experience by going through a battle. The inner struggle becomes the trigger for these things to be revealed.

The next blessing is the one that becomes the catalyst for personal change because tough personal battles force you to **ask the tough questions**. Questions that, maybe, you never wanted to know the answers to. On a recent conference call with a client, I was asked a question that I found very odd even for a coaching session. The client, who just had a brief brush with the IE of Doubt, asked if I believed he was a good person. I told him that it doesn't matter if I think he's a good person; what matters is if *he* thinks he's a good person. It's a question that he had a difficult time answering because, as we discovered, he had a warped view of what a good person is. As a result, he struggled with being a good enough person worthy of good things in his life and especially his business. Sadly, every time he would not experience the "good things" he expected, he would question his "goodness." His battle forced him to ask the tough question, "Do I believe that I am a good person?" He is now working on revamping his embedded belief of what a "good person" is.

Changing your perception about your circumstances, environment, and people around you is another blessing birthed from an IE struggle. The way you see those who support you, encourage you, and love you through your ordeal transforms how you see them moving forward. You no longer see them just as friends or "on paper" family but as allies in battle. There is a significant difference, by the way. You can have fairweather friends or on paper family. Still, they may not be the necessary allies you need while you're fighting for your spiritual, emotional, and mental life. The way you assess your current circumstances may change how you appreciate what you have, who you are, and your accomplishments. You may experience more gratitude and slow down long enough to enjoy life. You may learn not to sweat the small stuff so much. What a great blessing this is!

Consequently, battles compel you to **embrace a different set of actions**. In other words, the same ol' can no longer be the same ol'. Taking a hard look at what behaviors or habits need to be revamped is a positive thing. Establishing new disciplines and goal-achieving patterns also can be extremely beneficial to your overall success. The bottom line is that invisible enemies will continue to attack you if nothing that you do changes.

Finally, let me make one last exhortation to all of you. A scripture in the Bible asserts *(paraphrase)* not to be a hearer of the word but be a doer (James 1:22). Would you allow me to echo those same sentiments here? If you read this book and do nothing with what you've learned, then it would have been a waste of your time, money, and energy. The fact is, **YOU CAN** have more victories over your battles with invisible enemies. **YOU CAN** face your inner struggles head on more valiantly. However, **YOU MUST** choose daily to be a doer and not just a reader *(or hearer).* If you do, I can assure you more peace, joy, success, clarity, and freedom than you ever thought could exist for you!

"TRUE CHANGE ONLY COMES WHEN YOUR DESIRES OVERPOWER YOUR HURTS."©

REVIEWS

"Jay Maymi has written a powerful book that provides the reader with the tools to dig deep inside themselves to recognize, tackle, and to conquer life's inner struggle on the road to achieving the successes they desire. Very Inspirational!"

Alfred Titus, Jr., Speaker, Professor
Author of "Forward Motion:
The Keys to Progress and Success"
www.atitusconsulting.com

"Jay's book is a must-read. His insights into human behavior will surely hit home with every reader. It certainly did for me! Even if you don't think it applies to you (but it does), it is a must read just to help, and/or understand, friends, family, and coworkers."

Jamie Hargrove
Attorney/CPA, Co-founder/CEO, NetLaw

"Jay's book helps us all realize that we become what we think about: amazing or underwhelming. He skillfully helps us understand how thoughts, emotions, and actions can drag us down or catapult us beyond our wildest dreams. A powerful " How to" guide to give you the tools to hit full throttle and accomplish your goals."

Kelli Vrla, CSP
Engage YOUniversity.com
Kelliv.com

"Jay Maymi's writing style is easy to read and understand. This is a book that many will use to change their lives. Thank you for putting your fingers to the keyboard to bring forth this needed epistle. This is more than just a book. It is an epistle. It is an epistle to all who do not recognize that they win or lose the battle in their head before ever doing a thing physically. Bravo, sir."

Beverly F. Jones, C.H., MBA
Commanding Your Life Consultancy
The Silver Fox of Consciousness
www.commandingyourlife.com

"Jay Maymi has provided a rather straightforward and simple step by step road map. First, defining what is an invisible enemy is. Then, how to recognize your enemy's objective. Next, understanding when and how these can occur. Finally, modeling the Downward Spiral of the Enemies. In his book, he teaches you the Rules of Engagement and how to protect yourself and fight back. From a biblical perspective, I see it as putting on the Whole Armor of God (Ephesians 6:10 – 18). Of course, I could go on and on about what I see are the benefits of this book, but it is up to you to take the necessary steps. Read it once, twice, three times, or more, learn to recognize your invisible enemy, and then establish your battle plan. You will not regret it. I didn't."

Chaplain & Prof., Ron Carson, M.P.S., A.A.C.C
Lecture for the City University of New York
on Critical Thinking and Urban Sociology

"Jay's book is truly beyond impactful, powerful, and so real for just about anyone. A must read and great gift for the holiday. This book is a best seller for sure. This book wants me to scream, "bring it on, battles, what else do you have. I'm ready for you!" I'm going to re-read this very often. I will also recommend it to everyone I know. Thanks for writing this. I'm going to finish the year stronger than ever because of the book."

George Futterman, Prudential Financial
Million Dollar Round Table, President's Council
Financial Education Advocate- Speaker

"WOW!!! I can barely put into words how impressive, useful, and tangible this book will be for hundreds of thousands of people pursuing their dreams!!! A "must-have on me at all times resource" for anyone pursuing their dreams. Exceptional accuracy, humor, and eloquence delineating the Invisible Enemies of Success with applicable tools & techniques to WIN the battle."

Amber Schoenrock, The Money Duchess
www.moneyduchess.com

"My God! Jay Maymi has written an instant classic!"

Rosaki Akeem Hilt
Founder and CEO, Powerhouse Sales Academy
www.phsalesacademy.net

"Jay has written a book that everyone MUST HAVE & MUST READ!! It's a book to refer back to consistently to ensure that if any of the Invisible Enemies are launching a sneak attack, you will be ready. He teaches you how to launch a vigilante attack utilizing the IEDS strategies. I loved the deep dive Jay took in the book to dissect The Downward Spiral Model and each IE. "GIVE YOUR YESTERDAYS AN EVICTION NOTICE"... man, I LOVE THAT! This book truly is an EPIC GAME CHANGER. THANK YOU THANK YOU FOR WRITING IT."

Jeff Huggins, Partner
Synergy Financial Partners

"Battling Invisible Enemies is yet another amazing book by author Jay Maymi. It helps people from all walks of life identify and overcome the mental obstacles that hold many people from achieving true success. In this book, Jay does an incredible job bringing crystal-clear and powerful solutions to the many obstacles that may be keeping them from having the life that they have always wanted. This book is a must-read for anyone who is striving for that constant self-improvement in their life to take things to the next level."

John Benham, CEO and Founder
Vantage Financial Alliance

BE SURE TO SUBSCRIBE TO THESE PORTALS FOR MORE RESOURCES AND TRAINING:

FOR DAILY INSPIRATION, SHOP AT

WWW.ZAZZLE.COM/THEJAYMAYMI

MORE BOOKS FROM JAY MAYMI

Made in the USA
Monee, IL
15 February 2021